I Spy
with My Little
Eye
Minnesota

By Kathy-jo and Ed Wargin

Fun for all ages!

Sleeping Bear Press

We would like to express our thanks and appreciation to the Como Park Zoo and Conservatory in St. Paul, The International Wolf Center in Ely, the North American Bear Center in Ely, The Bemidji Chamber of Commerce, Split Rock Lighthouse State Park, The Minnesota State Fair, the Minnesota State Capitol in St. Paul, as well as Dale and Jeannine Saari of Palo for the use of a dock and antique lures.

This book is dedicated to Ernie and Rita Wallin of St. Paul.

Sleeping Bear Press™

315 E. Eisenhower Pkwy., Ste. 200
Ann Arbor, MI 48103
www.sleepingbearpress.com

© 2008 Sleeping Bear Press is an imprint of Gale, a part of Cengage Learning.

10 9 8 7 6 5 4 3

Library of Congress Cataloging-in-Publication Data

Wargin, Kathy-jo.
I spy with my little eye. Minnesota / written by Kathy-jo Wargin ;
photograghs by Ed Wargin.
p. cm.
Summary; "Each page includes two photos related to Minnesota. Using
poetic clues, readers try to spy the changes made from the original
photo on the left to the altered photo on the right. Subjects include
the Duluth Aerial Lift Bridge, the state capitol, the Como Zoo, and the
Minnesota State Fair"—Provided by publisher.
ISBN 978-1-58536-359-9
1. Minnesota—Juvenile literature. 2. Picture puzzles—Juvenile
literature. I. Wargin, Ed. II. Title. III. Title: Minnesota.
F606.3.W363 2008
977.6—dc22
2008012876

Printed by China Translation & Printing Services Limited, Guangdong Province, China. 3rd printing. 03/2010

I spy with my little eye, two pictures that look just the same.
An identical view isn't always what's true.
Find the changes to play this game.

Find
10
Changes

Now let's get started...

I spy with my little eye, changes to bright camping gear
change a lantern and bike, tasty food for a hike, flipped-out kayaks, and paddles to steer.

Find

24

Changes

Photo Fact: There are 72 state park and recreation areas in Minnesota and more than 5,700 state park campsites. With the establishment of Itasca State Park in 1891, Minnesota became the second state in the country to develop a state park system.

I spy with my little eye, a difference in dogs and more.
The brown eyes may change while the birds rearrange, and we paddle away from the shore.

Find
20
Changes

Photo Fact: The Boundary Waters Canoe Area Wilderness is a vast and pristine wilderness consisting of more than 1,000 lakes and streams with more than 1,500 miles of canoe routes. Located within the Superior National Forest, the BWCAW is more than 1 million acres in size and some of the largest animal residents are moose, black bears, and gray wolves.

I spy with my little eye, a lighthouse that sits above all.
From the base to the top, little changes won't stop, and a window looks out from the wall.

Find **10** Changes

Photo Fact: Split Rock Lighthouse State Park is situated on the north shore of Lake Superior, and is a favorite destination for visitors. It was completed in 1910 by the United States Lighthouse Service and was in operation until 1969. The Split Rock Cliff is 130 feet tall.

I spy with my little eye, Paul Bunyan and Babe the Blue Ox.
Changing grins and a nose, letters state where they pose, from the pockets right down to the socks.

BEMIDJI

PAUL
PUNYAN
1937

Photo Fact: This particular statue of Paul Bunyan and Babe is located in the city of Bemidji, near the shore of Lake Bemidji. The statue was built in 1937 and was placed on the National Register of Historic Places by the National Park Service in 1987.

I spy with my little eye, an affair that no matter the weather
brings mixed-up back ends and a smile to all friends, while a gopher says let's get together.

Find 21 Changes

I spy with my little eye, a view through a window and dome.
As four horses go by, underneath a blue sky, we know Minnesota's our home!

Find
15
Changes

Photo Fact: This familiar structure is the third building to act as Minnesota's state capitol. The first was located in St. Paul and destroyed by fire. The second, also in St. Paul, was too small. Sculptor Daniel Chester French designed the four golden horses, also known as the "quadriga." French also sculpted the statue of Abraham Lincoln in the Lincoln Memorial in Washington, D.C.

I spy with my little eye, a very long tail come undone.
Spot the changes in dots while the others change spots; we know two heads are better than one.

Find
15
Changes

I spy with my little eye, a farm that is ready for fall.
Change a pumpkin with eyes, pick some apples for pies, find a tractor for making the haul.

Find
20
Changes

Photo Fact: Pumpkins are a fruit of the gourd family and are 90% water. The University of Minnesota has long been home to one of the most successful fruit breeding programs in the country. Homegrown Minnesota apple varieties include Honeycrisp, Cortland, McIntosh, Haralson, Regent and more.

Minnesota Apples

I spy with my little eye, a port where the freighters pass through
with an aerial span going up is the plan, while the herring gulls change every view.

Find
14
Changes

Photo Fact: Duluth is a freshwater port and home to the Aerial Lift Bridge, which spans a canal put through a sandbar called Minnesota Point but commonly known as Park Point. The bridge was built in 1905 and upgraded in the 1920s. It was placed on the National Register of Historic Places in 1973.

I spy with my little eye, the changes in winter's wide view.
Watch for magical sticks, shiny blades that play tricks, missing pullers, and bells, and a shoe.

Find
18
Changes

Photo Fact: The average snowfall in Minnesota is nearly 60 inches per year. Skating, hockey, cross-country and downhill skiing as well as snowshoeing are favorite winter pastimes in Minnesota. There are more than 20,000 miles of snowmobile trails throughout the state.

I spy with my little eye, the lures of our best fishing scene.
Some are old, some are new, take the frog's point of view, change the color of lines blue to green.

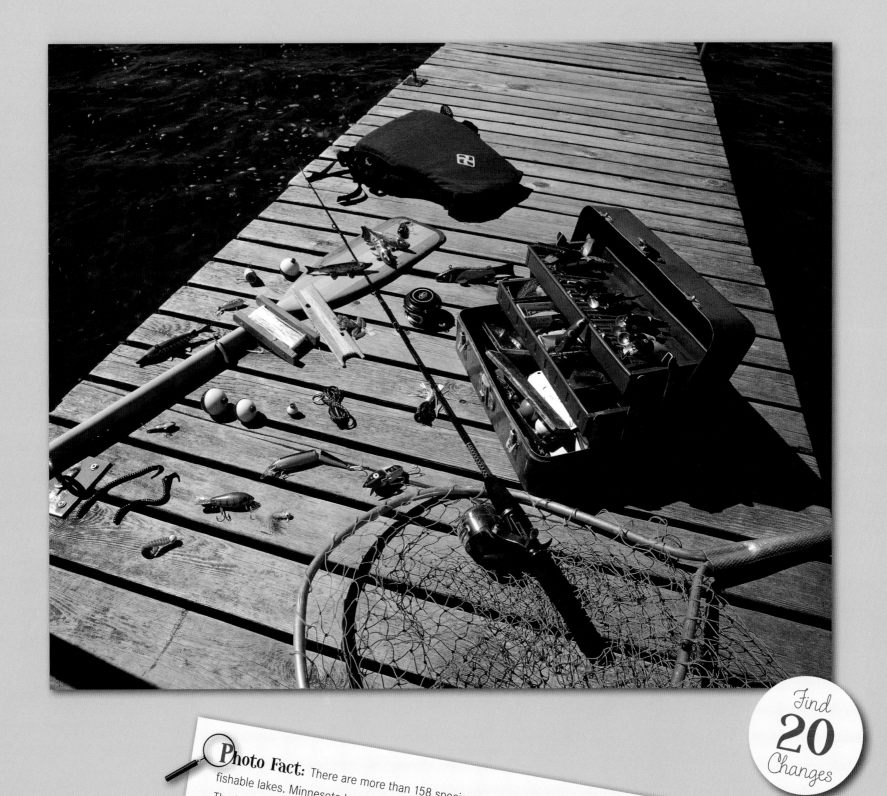

Photo Fact: There are more than 158 species of fish in Minnesota and more than 5,300 fishable lakes. Minnesota leads the nation in the number of fishing licenses sold per capita. The Minnesota state fish is the walleye.

I spy with my little eye, two scenes that look the same.
Balls disappear yet the goal remains clear, find the changes to win this game.

BASKETBALL!

Touchdown!

26

SCORE!

sweet shot!

GOAL!

HOCKEY!

GO TEAM

GAME DAY

SLAPSHOT!

53

FOOTBALL

GO TEAM

MINNESOTA

Find
26
Changes

Photo Fact: Professional football got its start in Minnesota with the Minneapolis Marines, a team that existed from 1905-1924. In 1993 the Minnesota North Stars moved to Dallas and became the Dallas Stars. When the American Basketball Association was launched in 1967, one of its charter teams was to be the Minnesota Muskies, which played in 1967-68 before moving south and becoming the Miami Floridians in 1968-69.

I spy with my little eye, tugboats and towers and more.
We can spot two "16"s where they speed in between, changing railings and ropes to the shore.

Find
15
Changes

Photo Fact: Boats like these have been and will continue to be familiar sights in Minnesota as they travel the waters of Lake Superior, the largest and deepest Great Lake. The United States Coast Guard Cutter *Sundew* was launched in Duluth, Minnesota in 1944. It served as an icebreaker as well as conducting search and rescue missions throughout the Great Lakes.

I spy with my little eye, a map that is one busy scene.
Look for changes in agates and loons near the shore, wild rice and arrows, state symbols and more.
From pinecones to prairies, this one is a test, but we love Minnesota — it's filled with the best!

Find
35
Changes

Photo Fact: The Minnesota state grain is wild rice. The state bird is the common loon. The state beverage is milk and the state tree, the Norway Pine, is not a native of Norway, but hails from Norway, Maine. Minnesota has one recreational boat for every six people. This is more than any other state in the country.

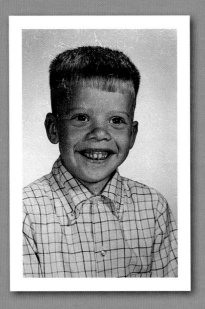
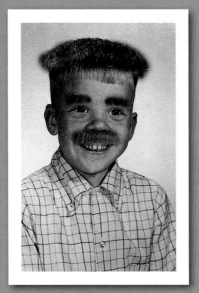

Ed Wargin is an award-winning landscape photographer well-known for his beautiful images from the Great Lakes region, including Michigan Notable Book Award winning books titled *Voelker's Pond, A Robert Traver Legacy; Legends of Light, A Michigan Lighthouse Portfolio;* as well as *Lake Michigan, A Photographic Portfolio.* He was born and raised in Duluth, Minnesota.

Author *Kathy-jo Wargin* is the best-selling author of more than thirty-five books, including *The Legend of Minnesota, The Voyageur's Paddle,* and *V is for Viking: A Minnesota Alphabet.* Although Ed and Kathy-jo have worked jointly on coffee-table books such as *The Great Lakes Cottage Book* and *Michigan, The Spirit of the Land, I Spy with My Little Eye Minnesota* is their first collaborative children's book about their home state, inspired and created by their mission to encourage children to notice the small details in the beauty that surrounds them everyday. Kathy-jo was born and raised in northern Minnesota, and the couple makes their home in Michigan with their son, Jake.